Conversation
Sparks

CONVERSATION
SPARKS

Trivia Worth
Talking About

BY RYAN CHAPMAN

CHRONICLE BOOKS

SAN FRANCISCO

Library of Congress Cataloging-in-Publication Data available.

ISBN 978-1-4521-4002-5

Manufactured in China.

Book Design by Neil Egan
Layout assistance by Tatiana Pavlova

Chronicle Books LLC
680 Second Street
San Francisco, CA 94107
www.chroniclebooks.com

10 9 8 7 6 5 4 3 2

TO CONVERSATIONALISTS
EVERYWHERE.

Introduction

SOCIAL SCIENTISTS CANNOT SAY FOR CERTAIN HOW MANY CONVERSATIONS YOU HAVE IN YOUR LIFETIME, BUT IT'S SOMEWHERE BETWEEN THREE DOZEN AND ONE MILLION.

AND WHO KNOWS HOW MANY OF THOSE ARE POINTLESS REMARKS ABOUT THE WEATHER?

THIS BOOK WILL ENSURE YOUR CONVERSATIONS ARE SPICED WITH A LITTLE EXTRA SOCIAL JALAPEÑO. (BY THE WAY, IF YOU'VE EATEN A REAL JALAPEÑO, DRINK MILK TO NEUTRALIZE THE HEAT— WATER JUST SPREADS IT AROUND.)

READ ON, ENJOY, AND DON'T BE SURPRISED IF YOU FIND YOURSELF THE CENTER OF THE PARTY.

THE GOLDEN GATE BRIDGE IS SO LARGE THAT A TEAM OF ALMOST 40 PAINTERS MUST CONSTANTLY RE-APPLY NEW COATS OF ITS ICONIC "INTERNATIONAL ORANGE" COLOR: BY THE TIME THEY'VE FINISHED ONE SIDE, THE SEA AIR HAS OXIDIZED THE OTHER.

PSYCHOLOGIST ELLIOT ARONSON TESTED "THE PRATFALL EFFECT" AND FOUND THAT WE LIKE PEOPLE MORE AFTER WITNESSING THEIR MINOR MISTAKES. THIS MIGHT EXPLAIN WHY WE DISLIKE PEOPLE WHO SEEM PERFECT.

SATELLITES FALL BACK TO EARTH AT A RATE OF ABOUT ONE PER DAY.

WILLARD WIGAN CREATES SCULPTURES THE SIZE OF HUMAN BLOOD CELLS. HE WORKS, NATURALLY, WITH A MICROSCOPE, AND HE'S LEARNED TO WORK IN-BETWEEN HEARTBEATS, LEST HIS PULSE MOVE HIS FINGER AND DESTROY THE ARTWORK.

THE AMERICAN INSTITUTE OF ARCHITECTS HONORED KANSAS CITY'S KEMPER ARENA WITH AN AWARD FOR DESIGN EXCELLENCE IN 1976, AND EVEN HELD THE AIA ANNUAL CONVENTION THERE IN 1979. THE DAY AFTER THE CONVENTION WRAPPED UP, THE ARENA'S ROOF COLLAPSED.

WEALTHY RUSSIANS HAVE FOUND A CLEVER, IF UNETHICAL, SOLUTION TO MOSCOW'S EPIC TRAFFIC JAMS: AMBULANCE TAXIS. FOR AROUND $200 AN HOUR, YOU'LL BE TAKEN THROUGH GRIDLOCK IN A REAL-LOOKING AMBULANCE WITH LIGHTS FLASHING AND SIREN WAILING.

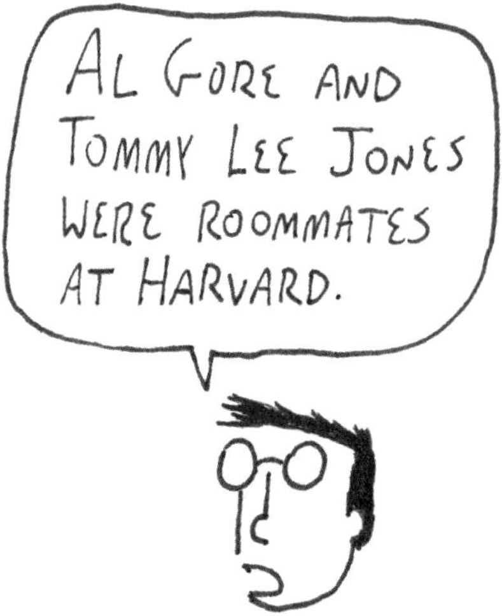
AL GORE AND TOMMY LEE JONES WERE ROOMMATES AT HARVARD.

ONE OF AMERICA'S ODDEST DISASTERS IS THE GREAT MOLASSES FLOOD OF 1919, WHICH KILLED 21 AND INJURED 150. MORE THAN 2 MILLION GALLONS SPREAD THROUGH BOSTON'S NORTH END NEIGHBORHOOD AFTER A STORAGE BANK BURST.

MEN ARE FOUR TIMES MORE LIKELY TO BE STRUCK BY LIGHTNING THAN WOMEN.

THE "YE" IN "YE OLDE PUB" IS ACTUALLY PRONOUNCED "THE": IT'S THE OLD ENGLISH LETTER "THORN," WHICH MAKES A "TH" SOUND.

In the early 1990s AT&T spent millions advertising 1-800-OPERATOR, its service for cheap long distance calls. Competitor MCI knew a lot of people misspell the word and made a ton of money with its secret alternative: 1-800-OPERATER.

THE MOON LOOKS THE SAME SIZE AS THE SUN, EVEN THOUGH IT'S 400 TIMES SMALLER. WHY? BECAUSE IT'S 400 TIMES CLOSER.

When Picasso visited Jean Cocteau, he spotted an old abstract painting of his he'd forgotten about. Cocteau replied that it wasn't a Picasso at all, but a forgery Cocteau had made. Picasso was impressed and signed "his" work.

THE EMPIRE STATE BUILDING ONCE HAD A DOCKING STATION FOR BLIMPS. IT HELPED RAISE THE ICONIC BUILDING'S HEIGHT TO JUST ABOVE THE NEARBY CHRYSLER BUILDING.

THE FIRST VIDEO UPLOADED TO YOUTUBE FEATURES COFOUNDER JAWED KARIM AT THE SAN DIEGO ZOO TALKING ABOUT ELEPHANT TRUNKS.

THE FIRST TV AD FOR A TOY WAS 1952's MR. POTATO HEAD, WHICH BECAME AN INSTANT HIT. CREATOR GEORGE LERNER INITIALLY HAD TROUBLE PITCHING THE IDEA: WITH WWII's RATIONS FRESH IN THE PUBLIC'S MIND, INVESTORS THOUGHT USING A POTATO AS A TOY WAS WASTEFUL.

THE CHARACTER LIMIT FOR TEXT MESSAGES IS KIND OF ARBITRARY. FRIEDHELM HILLEBRAND, WHO SET THE GLOBAL STANDARD, SIMPLY TYPED OUT SEVERAL QUESTIONS AND REPLIES, THEN COUNTED THE CHARACTER LENGTH. HE DECIDED THAT 160 CHARACTERS WAS ENOUGH.

WHT U UP 2?

THE MAN WHO VOICED SUPERMAN IN THE RADIO SHOW POPULARIZED KRYPTONITE IN JUNE 1943 AS A PLOT DEVICE TO PUT THE HERO IN A COMA. WHY? IT GAVE THE ACTOR A FEW DAYS OF VACATION.

87% OF WIKIPEDIA CONTRIBUTORS ARE MEN.
AND ACCORDING TO WIKIPEDIA, THEY ARE ALL CORRECT.

A GROUP OF OWLS IS CALLED A "PARLIAMENT."

THE WORKING TITLE
FOR THE VIDEO GAME
DOOM WAS IT'S GREEN
AND PISSED.

American colonists loved to toast themselves, toast one another, and toast the Queen. Historians estimate their annual consumption of alcohol was triple our modern intake.

THE PLEASURE CENTER IN THE BRAIN SPIKES WITH ACTIVITY IN EXPECTATION OF DRINKING WINE WE'RE TOLD IS EXPENSIVE, EVEN IF IN REALITY IT'S A CHEAP BOTTLE WITH A FAKE PRICE TAG.

SOME PEOPLE ARE BORN WITHOUT FINGERPRINTS, DUE TO A GENETIC CONDITION CALLED ADERMATOGLYPHIA.

On a film location, the shot setup before lunch is the "Orson Welles," the fourth-to-last shot of the day is the "Maya Angelou," and the last shot of the day is the "Martini Shot."

THE EMMYS AND THE OSCARS STILL USE A LAUGH TRACK TO "SWEETEN" THE AUDIENCE'S REACTION IN THE SEVEN-SECOND DELAY BETWEEN THE LIVE EVENT AND THE TV BROADCAST.

HA
HA
HA

THERE ARE MORE THAN A MILLION WORDS IN THE ENGLISH LANGUAGE, WITH A NEW ONE COINED EVERY 98 MINUTES.
LIKE SRSLY.
AND FOOD COMA.
AND SHVITZ.

THE MALE FACE CARDS IN A STANDARD DECK REPRESENT REAL PEOPLE: CHARLEMAGNE FOR THE KING OF HEARTS, JULIUS CAESAR FOR THE KING DIAMONDS, ALEXANDER THE GREAT FOR THE KING OF CLUBS, AND THE BIBLE'S KING DAVID FOR THE KING OF SPADES.

YOU HAVE AN AVERAGE OF 70,000 THOUGHTS PER DAY, THOUGH MANY OF THESE ARE THE SAME ONES FREQUENTLY REOCCURRING.
PICK UP MILK
CLEAN BATHROOM
GROW A BEARD
VISIT CANADA
PICK UP MILK

RUSSIA'S PETER THE GREAT ENFORCED A TAX ON BEARDS IN 1705. TAXPAYERS CARRIED A SILVER TOKEN BEARING THE PHRASE "THE BEARD IS A SUPERFLUOUS BURDEN."

NINTENDO'S MARIO WAS ORIGINALLY CALLED "JUMPMAN." HIS NEW NAME WAS COURTESY OF MARIO SEGALE, THE LANDLORD OF THE COMPANY'S U.S. OFFICE. HE FATEFULLY INTERRUPTED A MEETING OF NINTENDO EMPLOYEES BRAINSTORMING NAMES FOR THE AMERICAN RELEASE.

THE 4,000-YEAR-OLD CODE OF HAMMURABI PROSCRIBED BABYLONIAN LAW... AND THE PRICE OF BEER.

Animal crossings called "ecoducts" help wildlife traverse dangerous roads. The Netherlands is something of a pioneer: one bridge runs for over half a mile over a highway, a golf course, and a business park.

NIKE COFOUNDER PHIL KNIGHT PAID A STUDENT IN DESIGN SCHOOL $35 FOR THE FAMOUS SWOOSH LOGO. AFTER NIKE TOOK OFF, KNIGHT FOUND HER AND SAID THANKS WITH AN UNDISCLOSED AMOUNT OF STOCK.

LONDON CABBIES MUST PASS A TEST CALLED "THE KNOWLEDGE," MEMORIZING THE CITY'S 25,000 STREETS, LANDMARKS, PARKS, CHURCHES AND RESTAURANTS. IT USUALLY TAKE THREE YEARS AND TWELVE ATTEMPTS TO PASS.

WHEN THE <u>MONA LISA</u> WAS STOLEN FROM THE LOUVRE IN 1911, THE POLICE WERE DESPERATE FOR LEADS. ACTING ON A TIP, THEY ARRESTED AND INTERROGATED A 29-YEAR-OLD PABLO PICASSO. THEY LET HIM GO SOON AFTER.

HOTELS ARE FOR WIMPS. IN 2010, CHICAGO'S MUSEUM OF SCIENCE AND INDUSTRY ALLOWED ONE MAN TO SPEND AN ENTIRE MONTH IN A HOTEL-STYLE GLASS ENCLOSURE RIGHT IN THE CENTER OF THE BUILDING.

NARCISSISTS' CHARISMA TENDS TO WEAR OFF AFTER TWO-AND-A-HALF HOURS. SO IF YOU'RE EXTREMELY CHARMED BY YOUR DATE, WAIT UNTIL DESSERT BEFORE MAKING ANY BIG DECISIONS.

SURE, ESKIMOS HAVE 50 DIFFERENT WORDS FOR SNOW. BUT GERMANS HAVE 30 DIFFERENT WORDS FOR KISSING. I RECOMMEND TRYING <u>VERRATERKUSS</u>, THE "KISS OF A TRAITOR."

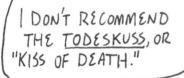

I DON'T RECOMMEND THE <u>TODESKUSS</u>, OR "KISS OF DEATH."

THE FIRST TIME THE WORDS "PREGNANT," "SEDUCE," AND "VIRGIN" APPEARED IN A HOLLYWOOD FILM WAS 1953's THE MOON IS BLUE. IT WAS PROMPTLY BANNED IN BOSTON AND DECRIED BY THE CATHOLIC CHURCH.

BEFORE 24-HOUR PROGRAMMING WAS STANDARD, MOST TV CHANNELS AIRED A TEST CARD DURING OFF HOURS. NETWORKS IN CHINA, AUSTRALIA, AND CANADA CAME UP WITH THE SAME ALTERNATIVE: A CAMERA POINTED AT A FISH TANK. HONG KONG'S "TELEFISION" EVEN BECAME A HIT, OUTPERFORMING PRIMETIME SHOWS.

Even though Spielberg shelved his planned <u>E.T.</u> sequel, the studio approved a novelization in 1985. <u>E.T.: The Book of the Green Planet</u> features E.T. returning to his home planet to be censured for his poor handling of his mission to Earth.

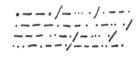

In 2002, <u>Sesame Street</u>'s Elmo testified before Congress asking for more music education in schools.

HOSPITALS OFTEN BEAR THE CADUCEUS SYMBOL OF TWO SNAKES WRAPPED AROUND A WINGED ROD, WHICH MANY THINK IS THE GREEK SYMBOL OF HEALTH AND MEDICINE. IT'S ACTUALLY THE IMAGE OF HERMES, THE GOD OF COMMERCE AND THIEVES.

THE MODERN CLIFFHANGER CAN BE TRACED TO THE SEASON-ENDING "WHO SHOT J.R.?" PLOT ON THE SHOW <u>DALLAS</u>. 83 MILLION PEOPLE TUNED IN FOR THE ANSWER ON NOV. 21, 1980.

IT WAS KRISTIN! HIS MISTRESS AND SISTER-IN-LAW!

The British crown claims ownership of the country's mute swans. Today, this is recognized in an annual "Swan Upping." The Queen's office oversees a swan count and health checkup for every swan living along the Thames.

In 1865, Joshua Coopersmith tried to sell an early version of the telephone around New York. He was promptly deemed a con artist and arrested for fraud, and newspapers reported that his claims of transmitting human voice over wires were patently impossible.

In 1900, Kodak issued instructional pamphlets with ubiquitous images of happy families smiling—expressions soon copied by customers, replacing the formal bearing of 19ᵀᴴ-century photographs.

ALFRED HITCHCOCK WAS SO WORRIED ABOUT PRESERVING THE SURPRISES IN _PSYCHO_ THAT HE BOUGHT ALL REMAINING COPIES OF ROBERT BLOCH'S ORIGINAL NOVEL AHEAD OF THE FILM PREMIERE.

BOB KANE WAS SITTING IN A PARK IN THE BRONX FACING EDGAR ALLAN POE'S OLD FARMHOUSE WHEN HE CAME UP WITH THE IDEA FOR BATMAN.

The popular <u>Where's Waldo?</u> books originated in England as <u>Where's Wally?</u> In fact, he goes by several names: Charlie in France, Holger in Denmark, Valdik in the Czech Republic, Vallu in Finland, Hugo in Sweden, and Ali in Turkey.

Some true facts about the author:

Ryan Chapman works in book publishing. He once played pool with Aziz Ansari. He has a mild allergy to dogs and ragweed. He hosts an infrequent literary trivia night for inebriated English majors. About 15% of his tweets @chapmanchapman are sarcastic lies. He lives in Brooklyn with his wife. Despite the allergy they want to adopt a dog.

Acknowledgments:

To Wynn, Neil, Lia, Michelle, and the entire Chronicle team, thanks for your masterful publishing alchemy, enthusiasm, and infectious joie de vivre.

And thanks to Rachel Fershleiser and Kate McKean for their encouragement, especially in the project's early days.

And a special thanks to Summer Smith, who is more interesting and witty than anything in this book. Or any others.